WILDLIFE SAFARI

Written by

Steve Pollock

Illustrated by

**Sheila Ratcliffe, Eric Tenney, Shelagh McNicholas,
Susan Harniess, Petra Stanton, Sandie Hill and Robin Lawrie**

Designed by

Teresa Foster

Edited by

Tony Potter

CONTENTS

About this book

All animals have to solve the same kinds of survival problems. Where to find the next meal? How to avoid becoming a meal? Where to build a home? Who to breed with? How to rear a family?

Not all animals can solve these problems in the same way. A kangaroo needs food just as much as a hungry shark. But they each have their own ways of finding and eating a meal.

Wildlife Safari lets you explore in detail how one specially chosen animal is adapted to deal with a survival problem. It then goes on to explain how other animals are adapted differently to solve the same problems.

Here are the ten specially chosen animals:

1 Movement – Cheetah

The cheetah is the fastest land animal, but what makes it such a fast runner?

2 Feeding – Kangaroo

Kangaroos eat nothing else but tough vegetation in the dry, dusty Australian outback – what helps them survive?

3 Attack and defence – Garden spider

How does this cunning killer hunt? And how do animals avoid being eaten?

4 Senses – Great white shark

How does this man-eating monster fish find its next victim?

5 Communication – Common frog

What is the best way of letting another frog know where you are?

6 Breeding – The stickleback

How does a male stickleback convince a female that he is the one for her?

7 Rearing young — Nile crocodile

What makes this savage reptile such a caring mother?

8 Homes — Meerkats

Where do a merry band of meerkats make their home?

9 Social life — Leafcutter ant

Why does the leafcutter ant need friends to fight off enemies?

10 Conservation — Barn owl

What has made this bird so common all over the world, but so rare in Britain?

What to look for in this book

The featured animal – shows you in detail how one particular animal manages to solve one particular problem.

You can toucan – fun activities you can do to find out more about how animals solve problems.

Animal profile card – gives you the details of each featured animal so you can see at a glance how the different animals compare.

These pictures show the size of the animal compared to a well-known object.

Quiz questions and answers – test your powers of observation and work out how other animals solve their problems.

You need to hold the book up to a mirror to read the answers to questions!

The Cheetah

The Cheetah runs very fast over short distances, just like a sprinter. Its sleek but muscular and powerful body is just the right shape for running at speed to catch prey such as gazelles and antelopes. Cheetahs' feet are like running shoes. They have grips and spikes to dig into the ground. The grips are special ridges on the animal's foot pads. The claws act as spikes. Its claws stay out all the time, like a dog's. Other cats' claws tuck away in special sheaths in their paws. Because of this, cheetahs are put in a group all of their own.

A long tail helps the cheetah keep its balance as it swerves after prey.

Big powerful leg muscles

A cheetah has a bendy back to keep its body springy as it sprints.

Good eyesight and hearing.

Name	Cheetah
Scientific name	Acinonyx jubatus
Where it lives	Africa, S. Asia, Middle East
Habitat	Open grasslands, scrub
Size	2m nose to tail, 70cm to shoulder
Feeding habits	Carnivore – eats small antelope
Senses	Very good eyesight and hearing
Breeding	3 babies on average. Female rears young on her own
Social life	Stay alone. Males sometimes form small groups.
Conservation	In danger. Only 25,000 left

The eyes point forwards to help the cheetah judge distances when chasing prey.

Claws

Cheetahs kill by gripping their prey by the throat. This stops the victim from breathing.

Paw

Moving in water

Moving in water is more difficult than moving on land or in air. Water resists movement much more than air. Fish are shaped to slip easily through the water. Think how much easier it is to swim than walk through water.

These fins stop the fish rolling over.

The fish uses these fins as brakes and to stop it tipping head over tail.

A fish swims by moving its tail from side to side very fast. This forces the fish forward through the water. The fins help it keep its balance and also act as brakes.

Flying

Only three groups of animals can fly: birds, insects and one kind of mammal – bats.

Birds are the masters of the air, from tiny humming- birds to soaring eagles. The hummingbird hovers in one place by beating its wings 65 times per second. Eagles glide and hardly move their wings at all.

Hopping and jumping

Frogs and kangaroos move on land by hopping. They are very different animals, but both have long back legs. The legs work like springs. With one push, the animal leaps into the air.

Strong muscles are at the top of the legs.

Leading a double life

Some land animals spend part of their life in water. How do they swim in water? Which part of the body do they use?

The parts which help the animal swim are coloured red in these pictures.

A crocodile swims by lashing its tail from side to side. The powerful tail has flat sides which help to push against the water.

A penguin swims by flying through the water. Its wings have become flippers.

The platypus, like the frog, has webbed feet. But it swims by paddling with its front feet, not its back feet.

A frog kicks with its back legs by pushing through the water. Webbing between the toes gives the frog an extra surface for pushing.

What is this animal doing?

This is a flying squirrel. It is not flying but gliding. Pieces of skin are stretched between the front and back legs. They make a kind of parachute to keep the squirrel in the air.

These animals are also gliders:

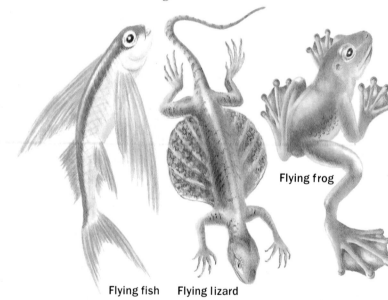

Flying fish   Flying lizard

Flying frog

Flying beetle

Ladybird, ladybird fly away home
Your house is on fire
And your children are gone.

Elytra

The ladybird is a kind of beetle. Beetles have two pairs of wings: a tough outer pair, called elytra, which form a case for a delicate pair underneath. You only see these when the insect flies.

The elytra are fixed in position when the beetle flies, a bit like the wings of an aeroplane.

Animal olympics

These pictures show some of the world's fastest insects, fish birds and other animals.

The longest frog jump is 3m.

Flying · 25kph frog

Horse · 50kph fly

Men · 62kph

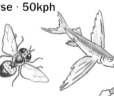

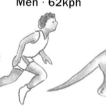

House · 1.8kph spider

Black · 17kph mamba

Women · 44kph

Flying fish · 56kph

Eastern grey · 64kph kangaroo

The longest kangaroo jump is 12.8m

You can toucan

Birds fly by flapping their wings, but the wings don't just move up and down. The pictures below show how the wings change and the feathers bend.
These steps show how to make a flick book to see the pigeon fly. You need eight pieces of stiff paper.

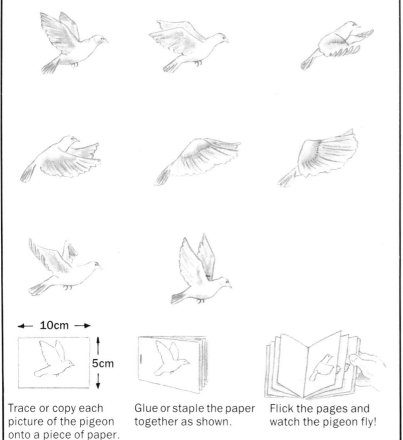

← 10cm →

5cm

Trace or copy each picture of the pigeon onto a piece of paper.

Glue or staple the paper together as shown.

Flick the pages and watch the pigeon fly!

Lots of legs

All these animals are arthropods. Arthropod means jointed limb. Different kinds have different numbers of legs. Count the arthopods' legs below to see which are in the same group.

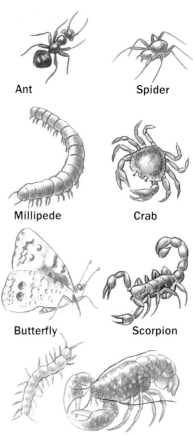

Ant

Spider

Millipede

Crab

Butterfly

Scorpion

Centipede

Lobster

Group	Number of legs
Insects	6
Spiders	8
Crabs	10
Millipedes	more than 10

Answers

Ant and butterfly
Spider and scorpion
Crab and lobster
Millipede and centipede

Peregrine falcon · 360kph

Greyhound · 66kph

Ostrich · 72kph

Cheetah · 104kph

The Kangaroo

There are several kinds of kangaroos. This picture shows a red kangaroo, which lives on the open plains of Australia. Its way of life is similar to an antelope on the African plains. Both animals live in groups, can run fast to escape danger, and eat plants such as grass. Animals which eat plants are called herbivores.

A Kangaroo's teeth work like those of most other herbivores. There are long, pointed teeth at the front used for cutting the grass. Then there is a gap until the back, or cheek, teeth. These grind the grass in a circular motion ready to be swallowed.

Chewing the cud

Grass has little goodness and is difficult to digest. Many herbivores, such as cows, chew the cud to help digest their food. Animals which chew the cud have large stomachs with several parts. The steps below show how this works.

Eyes at the side of the head help the kangaroo keep a look-out for danger when feeding.

The kangaroo quickly hops away from danger with its long, powerful back legs.

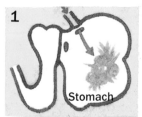

1

Stomach

The meal is chewed and swallowed. It stays in the stomach for a while.

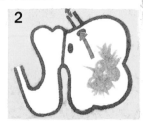

2

After a time, the animal brings up the meal for a second chew.

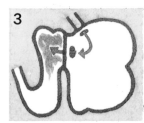

3

Now the food is ready to go to another part of the stomach to be digested.

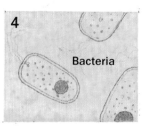

4

Bacteria

Microscopic germs inside the stomach, called bacteria, help the digestion.

Name:	Red Kangaroo
Scientific name:	Macropus rufus
Where it lives	Australia
Habitat	Open, dry grasslands
Size:	Head – body 165cm
	Tail 107cm
Feeding habits:	Herbivore – grasses and the leaves of shrubs
Senses:	Hearing and eyesight are best
Breeding	All year round. The baby takes 5 weeks to be born, but grows for another 235 days in its mother's pouch.
Social life:	Lives in groups of 2-10
Conservation:	Common, with hunting controlled

Feeding

Animals are divided into three main groups depending on what they eat. All of them have their own special ways of finding, eating and digesting food.

Plant eating animals are called herbivores. Antelopes, snails, rabbits, hummingbirds and caterpillars are all herbivores.

Meat eating animals are called carnivores. Lions, eagles, spiders, sharks and sea anemones are all carnivores.

Animals which eat both plants and meat are called omnivores. Pigs, rats and ourselves are all omnivores.

Hungry herbivores

Different parts of a plant are used in different ways by herbivores.

The leaves, stem and bark have the least goodness. But browsing animals such as deer, antelope, elephant and giraffe find this a tasty food.

The fruits on a plant can be tasty and might be eaten by monkeys or birds.

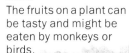

The flowers contain pollen and nectar. These are the favourite food of animals such as bees, bats and humming birds.

The seeds have the most goodness. They are eaten by birds and different kinds of rodents such as squirrels and mice.

Killing carnivores

Carnivores eat other animals. They must catch and kill their food before eating it, using many cunning tricks and skills.

Sharks have powerful jaws and sharp teeth to slice through their prey.

Birds of prey pounce on their victims.

Vultures eat the flesh of animals that have already died. They are called carrion eaters.

Omnivores

Ominivores often have a very varied diet. Bears, for example, eat just about anything – mice, fish, grass, nuts, honey and even people's lunches!

Feeding on the African savannah

This picture shows some of the animals that live on the plains of Africa. They are all eating something. See if you can work out which are the herbivores, which are the carnivores and which are omnivores.

5 Vultures

3 Elephant

4 Lion

2 Antelope

1 Weaver bird

6 Dung beetle

You can toucan

You can find out what animals eat by going out to watch them. Birds are probably the easiest to see. If you have a bird table, you could put different foods out to see which kinds of birds eat which kinds of food. You can also make your own fun feeders, like the one in this picture.

String

Holes cut out

Nuts and cereal

Old plastic fizzy drink bottle

Blue-tit

Answers

1 Herbivore — eating grass seeds.
2 Herbivore — grazing on grass.
3 Herbivore — eating the leaves and branches of a tree.
4 Carnivore — about to kill an antelope.
5 Carnivore — eating an already dead animal, which makes it a carrion eater.
6 Herbivore — eating second-hand vegetation (elephant dung).

Thorny problem

What four things does this giraffe have which will help it eat leaves growing in thorny trees?

Bird beaks

Try and match the shape of these birds' beaks with the pictures of the tools and the descriptions of what they do. The beaks work in the same way as the tools they match.

1 Darter

Dagger

Nut cracker

2 Tree creeper

Tea-strainer

3 Flamingo

4 Macaw

Tweezers

Meat cleaver

5 Eagle

A Probes with a long beak for insects in tree bark.

B Tears at flesh with a powerful hooked beak.

C Stabs fish with its beak.

D Strains tiny plants and animals from the water with its beak.

E Cracks open nuts and seeds with its powerful beak.

Answers

1C Dagger 2A Tweezers 3D Tea-strainer 4E Nut cracker 5B Meat cleaver

Answers

1 A long neck.
2 Long eye lashes to protect its eyes.
3 Nostrils that can close completely.
4 Floppy, hairy lips and a long tongue.

Gulp!

Snakes swallow their food whole. The meal gradually goes down the snake until it is completely gone – including the bones!Owls eat in the same way, but they bring up, or regurgitate, any bones, fur or feathers as a small pellet. You can sometimes find these near trees where owls live.

Grazers and browsers

Which rhinoceros makes the best lawn mower? Look at the shape of their lips. The white rhinoceros has a flat, wide upper lip for grazing grass. The black rhinoceros has a pointed, twisting upper lip for browsing on leaves and twigs. The white rhinoceros would make the best lawn mower!

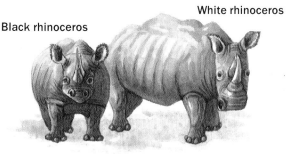

White rhinoceros

Black rhinoceros

Garden Spider

The garden spider is an expert hunter.
First it builds a trap – a fine silk web,
which it spins with silk-making glands.
And then it waits…

The spider's jaws produce venom that paralyses and sometimes kills small insects.

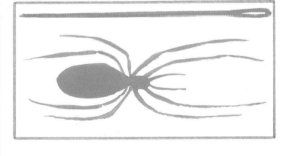

Name:	Garden spider
Scientific name:	Araneus diadenatus
Where it lives:	Found all over Europe
Habitat:	Woods, heaths and gardens
Size:	Female – 12mm / Male – 8mm
Feeding habits:	Carnivore – eats insects caught in its web. Web can reach 40cm in diameter.
Senses:	Good eyesight and sense of touch.
Breeding:	Female lays 300-800 eggs in a batch. Up to six batches. She spins a silky cocoon around the eggs.
Social life:	Solitary
Conservation:	Very common

How the spider hunts

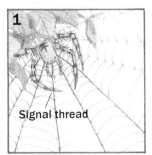

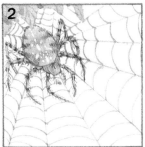

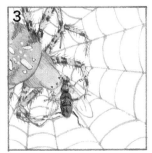

The spider sits and waits for a victim, holding on to a thread called the signal thread.

When an insect lands in the web its movements vibrate the signal thread. Feeling these vibrations, the spider rushes out.

The insect is bitten with poisonous jaws. This paralyses the victim so that the spider can wrap it in a parcel of silk.

Depending on how hungry it feels, the spider either eats its meal there or stores it for later.

Trap door spider

The trap door spider uses a different technique to catch its prey. It lives in an underground burrow, which has a trap door. When an insect passes close by, the spider rushes out and pulls it into its burrow.

Ant lion

Another trapper is the ant lion, it lives at the bottom of a sand pit with its long jaws sticking out of the top. Any small insect that falls in to the hole can't get out because of its slippery sides. It slides down to the waiting jaws of the ant lion.

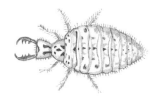

Patience pays

There are some animals that just lie in wait and don't use a trap. They stay well hidden because they are camouflaged. This flower mantis, for example, looks just like its background. This helps it in two ways. Firstly, it can stay hidden, ready to attack any insect which mistakes it for a flower. Secondly, it helps the flower mantis to avoid being eaten by a predator.

The next page shows some of the ways that different animals avoid being eaten.

Squirt!

The archer fish has a special way of attacking its prey. It squirts a jet of water from its mouth to knock insects from leaves dangling over the river. When the insect falls in the water, the archer fish gobbles it up.

Safety in numbers

Staying together in a large group gives each animal a better chance of survival. The patterns on these zebras make it difficult for a lion to see which animal to grab.

A sting in the tail

One of these scorpions has a more deadly sting than the other. Can you work out which one? Look at the claws. A jungle scorpion's strong claws are used as well as its sting to kill prey. A desert scorpion has only weak claws, so it needs to use a strong venom in its sting to kill its prey. So the desert scorpion has the deadlier sting – worth remembering the next time you are in the desert!

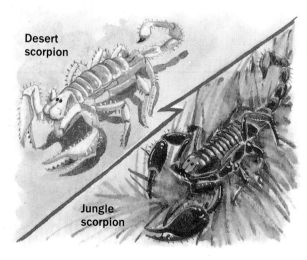

Desert scorpion

Jungle scorpion

Find the hidden insects

How many insects can you see here? Many animals are camouflaged. They are shaped or coloured to help them match the backgrounds where they live. This makes them much more difficult to see.

Answer

There are five insects

You can toucan

Many animals live together in large groups for protection. You can test whether the expression, "safety in numbers" is true. Imagine that you are the predator and fifteen dried peas are your prey. Now throw a single dried pea in the air and catch it. That was easy. Now try to do the same with fifteen peas. How many of them did you manage to catch and how many escaped?

You can test camouflage as well. You need five green, five blue, five red and five yellow cocktail sticks or plastic counters. Throw them into grass. Now find them. Which colour did you find first? How long did you take to find the green ones? What else, apart from their colour, makes them difficult to find in the grass?

Pretty and deadly

The bright colours on these animals is a warning – touch me and something nasty might happen to you. The arrow poison frog is covered in poisonous slime. It gets its name from the way its poison is used to tip the arrows of some South American Indians.

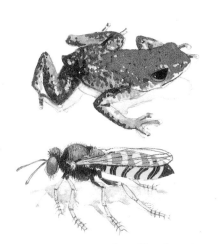

The wasp is not so deadly, but just as nasty in its own way. If any animal tries to grab the wasp it risks being stung. Animals soon learn to avoid anything with black and yellow stripes.

Watch out!

Work out what these animals use to defend themselves against attack.

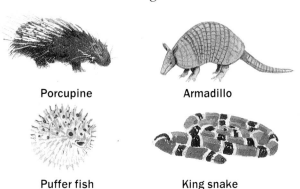

Porcupine   Armadillo

Puffer fish   King snake

Answers

Porcupine A porcupine uses its sharp spines. Its black and white colour may also act as a warning showing attackers that it is dangerous.

Armadillo Armadillos have a very hard skin for protection. This species can curl up its body into a ball and cover up all the soft part of its body.

Puffer fish This fish fills up with water and changes its size. It gets much bigger very quickly. It is too much of a mouthful and too spiny for most attackers.

King snake A snake's bright colours warn other animals that it is dangerous. But this snake is cheating – it is only pretending to be a dangerous animal. In fact, it is quite harmless. This tactic is called mimicry.

Great White Shark

Sharks have a very good sense of smell, which they use to find their food. The great white shark is a carnivore. It feeds on other fish and sea mammals such as seals. It will even attack and eat people, so it is also called the man–eater – it was the shark shown in the film "Jaws".

Smell and taste are the shark's best senses. Some sharks can smell the blood of injured prey from several kilometers away.

Some sharks have an extra sense that scientists do not understand very well. It can sense tiny amounts of electricity made by animals. This helps the shark to find small animals to eat, buried in the sea bed.

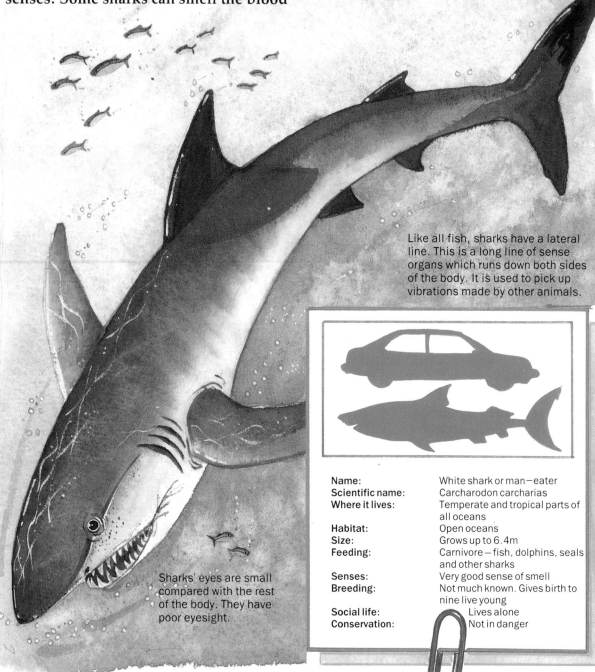

Like all fish, sharks have a lateral line. This is a long line of sense organs which runs down both sides of the body. It is used to pick up vibrations made by other animals.

Sharks' eyes are small compared with the rest of the body. They have poor eyesight.

Name:	White shark or man–eater
Scientific name:	Carcharodon carcharias
Where it lives:	Temperate and tropical parts of all oceans
Habitat:	Open oceans
Size:	Grows up to 6.4m
Feeding:	Carnivore – fish, dolphins, seals and other sharks
Senses:	Very good sense of smell
Breeding:	Not much known. Gives birth to nine live young
Social life:	Lives alone
Conservation:	Not in danger

Animal senses

There are five main senses: seeing, hearing, touching, tasting and smelling.

Some senses are more important than others to different animals.

Sight is probably our most important sense. You could test to see if this is true by asking people which sense they would most hate to lose.

A dog understands its world by smelling it. You can see this by watching a dog sniff where other dogs have been.

Sight is not very useful to a mole, which lives underground. It feels its way around instead, so it has a good sense of touch in its whiskers and tail.

Sense organs

The parts of its body that an animal uses for sensing are called the sense organs. The eyes, ears, skin, nose and tongue are all sense organs. Most animals have their main sense organs at the front of their body. Other animals, with special ways of life, have sense organs arranged differently. See where the animals in the picture below have their sense organs arranged to suit life in the water.

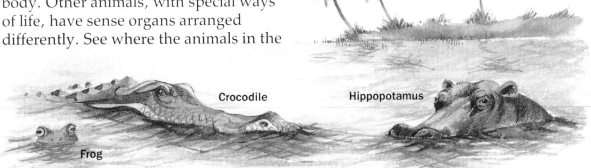

Crocodile

Hippopotamus

Frog

Strange senses

Some animals have different kinds of senses to find out about their world. Dolphins, many bats and the South American oilbird, for example, use a special hearing called echo-location to find their way around. The picture on the right shows how this works.

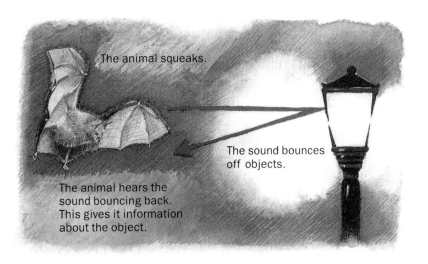

The animal squeaks.

The sound bounces off objects.

The animal hears the sound bouncing back. This gives it information about the object.

Making sense

Here is a rattlesnake's head. It is packed with sense organs. Its tongue flicks in and out all the time and picks up chemicals floating around in the air. These are passed to a special organ called the Jacobson's organ. This checks the chemicals and helps the snake find out if it is near something tasty to eat.

Rattlesnakes are nocturnal animals. Their pupils close to a slit like a cat's eyes during the day. There is a pit in front of each eye which is a heat-sensing organ. This is used to feel the heat given off by prey in the dark, such as mice and rats.

Snakes have one sense organ missing. They have no ears, so they are deaf. Snakes do feel vibrations through their bodies.

A shocking sense

The electric eel from South America uses electricity to find its way around in the muddy waters where it lives. It surrounds itself with electricity and can tell if a fish enters the area. A hungry eel will stun the fish with a powerful electric shock and then eat it. The shock is strong enough to kill a person.

You can toucan

Here are some things to do to test your sense of hearing.

Put some objects in tins – things such as nails, rubbers, marbles and stones. Shake the tins and see if your friends can guess what is inside them.

Try this test to see whether people's hearing gets better or worse as they get older. Position a watch with a tick at the end of a metre ruler. Hold the other end close to someone's ear and gradually slide the watch long the ruler. Try this with people of different ages and see who can hear the tick furthest away.

Use your senses!

Below are photographs of different animals, showing their sense organs. You can usually reckon that the larger the organ is compared to the rest of the animal's body, the more important it is. Look carefully at the animals and see if you can work out which senses are most important for each animal.

1 Male moth

2 Elephant

3 Jackal

4 Centipede

Answers

3 Nose. The long face and wet nose show that smell is important. Hearing is also important to a jackal.

4 Touch. The centipede has a good sense of touch all over its body so it can squeeze into tight cracks to hide.

1 Antennae. These pick up the chemical messages sent by females at breeding time.

2 Ears. Hearing is important, but the tip of the trunk is very sensitive too.

In colour

Not all animals can see in colour. Some only see shades of grey between black and white. Often, those that see in colour are very colourful themselves. Which of these animals do you think can see in colour?

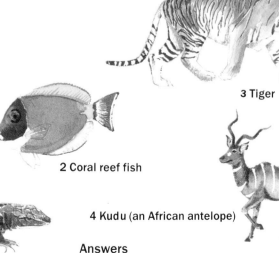

3 Tiger

2 Coral reef fish

4 Kudu (an African antelope)

1 Agama lizard

Answers

1 Yes   2 Yes   3 No   4 No

Frogs

Frogs are well known for the croaking sounds they make. Croaking is the way in which frogs communicate with one another. In the breeding season male frogs and toads croak to attract females.

Some kinds of frogs extend their throats by filling them full of air – sometimes so much that it looks like a balloon. With its throat blown out like this the frog can communicate with other frogs.

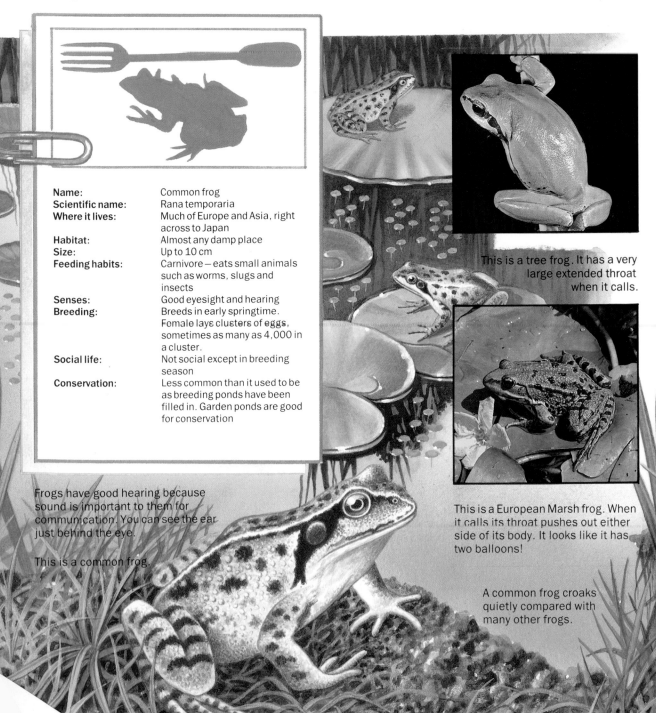

Name:	Common frog
Scientific name:	Rana temporaria
Where it lives:	Much of Europe and Asia, right across to Japan
Habitat:	Almost any damp place
Size:	Up to 10 cm
Feeding habits:	Carnivore – eats small animals such as worms, slugs and insects
Senses:	Good eyesight and hearing
Breeding:	Breeds in early springtime. Female lays clusters of eggs, sometimes as many as 4,000 in a cluster.
Social life:	Not social except in breeding season
Conservation:	Less common than it used to be as breeding ponds have been filled in. Garden ponds are good for conservation

This is a tree frog. It has a very large extended throat when it calls.

Frogs have good hearing because sound is important to them for communication. You can see the ear just behind the eye.

This is a common frog.

This is a European Marsh frog. When it calls its throat pushes out either side of its body. It looks like it has two balloons!

A common frog croaks quietly compared with many other frogs.

Animal language

Animals do not speak a language, but they communicate with each other using a whole range of different signals. The signals they use and recognize depend on their senses – of hearing, seeing, feeling, tasting and smelling. Animals usually make signals to communicate with other members of their own species. But some animals signal to other species to warn them off.

Here are some of the signals which we understand and which animals use in similar ways to communicate with each other.

Which team?

Which sex?

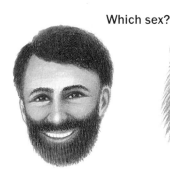

Football players and coral fish both recognize members of their own kind by the particular patterns on their bodies.

A male lion looks different from a lioness because he has a mane of hair. It is a bit like a man's beard. Only male lions have a mane and only men can grow a beard.

Who is boss?

It is important to be able to recognize your leader. Only the mandrill leader is brightly coloured. Sailors recognize an admiral because of his special uniform and colours.

Whose place?

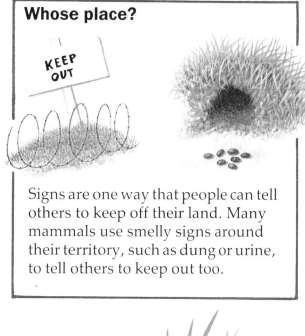

KEEP OUT

Signs are one way that people can tell others to keep off their land. Many mammals use smelly signs around their territory, such as dung or urine, to tell others to keep out too.

Dancing bees

Worker bees communicate by dancing. Worker bees can tell others where and how far away food is. If the food is within 50 metres of the hives, it does a round dance. If the food is further, it does a waggle dance. Its movements also tell the other bees the direction in which they must fly to find the food.

Waggle dance

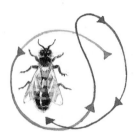

Round dance

Give us a kiss

Prairie dogs (also called marmots) live in a network of underground burrows, often several hundred at a time. When two prairie dogs meet, they kiss to recognize each other. If they are from the same group they start grooming one another. If they are from a different group they may fight.

You can toucan

People show their moods by making faces. Some animals, like the wolf, do much the same. See if you can match the human expressions to the wolf's.

A
B
C

1
2
3

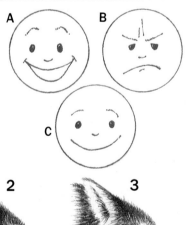

Answers A 2 Happy B 3 Angry C 1 Content

Climbing a tree?

The bush dog from South America has a special gland under its tail. It leaves a smelly message on trees and rocks for other bush dogs to smell. It even does a hand-stand to get its message high up!

Warning signals

The first deer to spot danger runs away. As it escapes the white underside of its tail is seen by the others in the herd. This is a warning that danger is near.

One dwarf mongoose stays on guard duty, whilst the others carry on feeding. When the guard sees an attack coming from the sky it calls a warning sound. A different sound is made when the attack is from the ground.

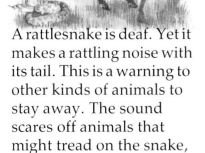

A rattlesnake is deaf. Yet it makes a rattling noise with its tail. This is a warning to other kinds of animals to stay away. The sound scares off animals that might tread on the snake, such as horses and bison.

Long distance calls

Grass hoppers live in long grass, so they find it difficult to see one another. They communicate by rubbing their hind legs together to make a rasping noise. This is called stridulating. Different species make different noises. They recognize one another from the particular noise that they make.

People shout when they cannot be seen, but want to be noticed. Animals do the same. In a tropical forest full of trees it is difficult to see far or to be seen. So gibbons from Asia, and howler monkeys from South America communicate by calling very loudly. Both species fill up their throats with air, which makes the noise sound much louder.

Many kinds of whales make noises. Sounds travel well through water, often hundreds of kilometers, so distant whales can still keep in touch. It is thought that whales can tell one another where they are by producing a whole range of noises, from high pitched squeals down to very deep grunts.

The Stickleback

At a certain time of the year a male stickleback's underneath turns bright red. This is a signal to female sticklebacks that he is ready to breed. He makes a special nest for females to lay their eggs in from bits of weed. But before they lay their eggs, the male stickleback has to court the females.

1 When he sees a female he swims nearby, doing a zig-zag dance.

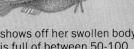

A male stickleback may breed with five different females.

2 She shows off her swollen body which is full of between 50-100 eggs.

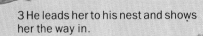

3 He leads her to his nest and shows her the way in.

4 She goes in and he prods her with his snout, making her lay her eggs.

5 She wriggles out. The male swims into the nest and squirts sperm over the eggs.

6 He then chases the female away, but stays with the eggs to keep them safe.

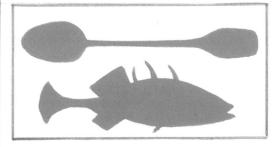

Name:	Three-spine stickleback
Scientific name:	Gasterosteus aculeatus
Where it lives:	In Europe, Eurasia, North America
Habitat:	Fresh water – ditches, lakes, rivers, brackish water and the sea
Size:	10cm
Feeding habitat:	Carnivore – eats small animals
Senses:	Eyesight is very good
Breeding:	Male builds a nest and protects the eggs
Social life:	Males are territorial in the breeding season
Conservation:	Very common. Not in any real danger

Breeding

Reproduction is the name scientists give to breeding – the way in which animals make their young.

Breeding often starts with courtship. This helps animals to choose the right partner. During courtship, males and females often change the way they normally behave towards each other. They may even change their appearance to be more attractive to the opposite sex.

The female glow-worm on the left attracts males with a greenish light at the tip of her body.

This male crested newt attracts females by changing his skin to a very bright colour.

Mating

After courtship the male and female are ready to mate. Mating is the joining up of the male's sex cells, the sperms, and the female's sex cells, the eggs. When a sperm touches an egg, the egg will grow. This is called fertilization. Once fertilization happens a new individual begins to grow and develop.

Animals living in water, such as jellyfish, fish and frogs, fertilize their eggs outside of their bodies. The sperms are released by the male into the water around the eggs.

Male mammals, some male birds and reptiles fertilize their eggs inside the female. Male mammals have a special part, called the penis, for putting sperm into the female's body.

A male lion mating with a female lion.

A male tortoise mating with a female tortoise.

In the breeding season a male frog grips a female frog for several days.

Fan-tastic!

Male peacocks display their fan of back feathers to attract females. The bird with the most magnificent feathers is the healthiest, so a female will mate with him to produce strong young.

Dancing with death

A male scorpion grabs a female by her pincers to dance with her. During the dance she picks up sperms left earlier on the ground by the male. The sperms mix with the female's eggs and make them grow.

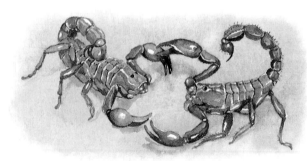

Robin

In the breeding season, a male robin claims an area as his own. This area is called a territory. The robin sings in the morning and evening to warn other robins where the boundaries are. Many animals have a territory where they breed and rear young. This picture shows the boundaries of two robins' territories in some gardens.

In the pink

A female baboon's bright pink, swollen bottom is a message to males that she is ready to breed. She shows off her bottom to the males in the troop, so that they mate with her.

Territory of robin A

Territory of robin B

Stags

Each year in the breeding season, the male red deer, called a stag, grows a new set of antlers. He uses them as weapons to fight off other stags and chase them away. The winner keeps a whole herd of females and mates with them. In this way only the healthiest, strongest males are able to breed.

You can toucan

Frogs breed by laying hundreds of eggs, called frog spawn. The eggs gradually turn into tadpoles and then into frogs. This process is called metamorphosis.

You can make a diary of the changes by collecting some frog spawn, keeping it in a tank with water and watching what happens.

Each number shows the stages the tadpoles will go through. See if you can work out how many weeks each stage takes and note in your diary what happens.

Some tadpoles will develop more quickly than others.

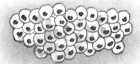

Day 1
The eggs are fertilized and float to the surface.

Day 5-10
The little black dots in the eggs become comma shapes.

Day 10
Little tadpoles start to hatch and hang on to the eggs or nearby pond weed.

Day 11-14
You can begin to see gills at the side of the tadpole's head. You may need a magnifying glass to see them properly.

Day 15-28
The body and tail start to form. The gills disappear under a flap of skin which grows over them.

Week 4-8
You can see the first signs of back legs growing.

Week 8-12
Over the next few weeks the tadpole gets bigger and begins to breathe with lungs. It starts to eat pond animals rather than plants. At the end of this time, the front legs begin to grow.

Week 12-16
The tadpole sheds its skin, the tail begins to shorten and it looks like a small frog.

Week 16
The young frog crawls out of the water and the tail stump disappears. The frog will live in damp vegetation and eat insects and other small animals.

Crocodiles

The female Nile crocodile digs a flask shaped hole in the ground, carefully lays her eggs in it, then covers them with sand. She stands guard over her nest for three months until the babies hatch. They make loud, grunting noises to let her know they are ready. The female hears them and digs out the young crocodiles.

The mother gently cracks open any eggs that have not hatched with her mouth, freeing the baby crocodiles. She then carries the babies in a special pouch in her mouth to a nursery area. Here she spends another three months guarding her young. All this care is necessary because crocodile eggs are eaten by predators – animals who dig them up and eat them. Baby crocodiles make a tasty meal for big lizards, birds and foxes, so their mother's care helps them survive.

The male crocodile takes no part in caring for the young crocodiles.

Name:	Nile Crocodile
Scientific name:	Crocodylus niloticus
Where it lives:	Africa
Habitat:	Near ponds, rivers and lakes
Size:	Grows between 4m-5m long
Feeding habits:	Carnivore – feeds on any form of meat
Senses:	Good hearing and eye sight
Breeding:	Digs a hole in which the female lays between 30-100 eggs. Incubation takes about three months
Social life:	No social organization, but often found together
Conservation:	Vulnerable. Hunted for its skin

Good mothers

It is not just the Nile crocodile that makes a good mother. These animals all make good parents because they take care of their young:

Mammals

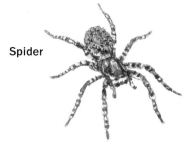
Spider

Birds

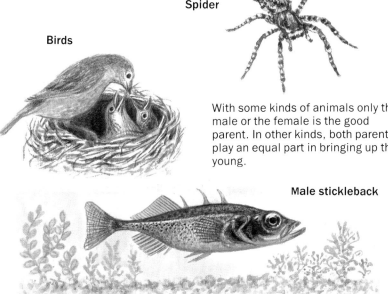

With some kinds of animals only the male or the female is the good parent. In other kinds, both parents play an equal part in bringing up the young.

Male stickleback

Scorpion

Good parents put a lot of effort into caring for their eggs and young. Some build a special nest for protection. Others, like the scorpion, carry their babies wherever they go.

How many babies?

Some animals have only a few eggs or babies and so take a great deal of care of them, often over a long period of time. They can only do this for a small number of babies.

Orang-utans take good care of their babies

From the millions of eggs produced by the cod perhaps only two will grow up to become parents themselves.

Other animals show no care at all. The common frog, many fish and insects lay hundreds of eggs, for example. Some, such as the cod, lay millions. Once the eggs are laid the parents show no further interest.

Many eggs and young are killed and eaten by other animals, so it is important that huge numbers are born so that a few can survive.

Eggstraordinary

All the animals in the pictures below carry their babies around until they are able to survive alone. See if you can think of any other animals which do the same thing.

Midwife toad

The male midwife toad wraps the fertilized eggs around his legs. He carries them everywhere he goes until they hatch.

Water Bug

The female giant water bug lays her eggs on the back of a male. He carries them around with him until they hatch after three weeks.

Marmoset

The male marmoset carries his young everywhere he goes. He hands them over to the female when it is feeding time.

Spider

The female wolf spider carries a cocoon of eggs everywhere she goes. When the baby spiders hatch out they ride on their mother's back for a time.

Cichlid fish

Some female cichlid fish protect their eggs by keeping them in their mouth. Even after they have hatched, the baby fish escape danger by swimming back into their mother's mouth.

Feeding time

Animals that take a lot of care of their babies usually produce or gather food for them. The discus fish goes one better – it is covered in edible slime! Young discus fish nibble and eat this slime when they first hatch.

Birds, like this owl, bring food to their youngsters. Some birds eat the food first, then bring it up for the babies to eat.

All female mammals, like this pig, produce milk to feed their young. The milk is made in special glands called mammary glands.

Big babies

Some baby mammals take a long time to grow inside the mother. This time is called the gestation period. The blue whale, the world's biggest mammal, has a gestation period of 21 months!

Cry babies

Some baby animals are more dependent than others. Compare these mammals and birds. They have all recently hatched or been born. Which ones do you think would need the most parental care?

Young mice

Pheasant chick

Blackbird chicks

Young antelope

Marsupial mothers

Marsupials are a special group of mammals that live mostly in Australia. Female marsupials, like the kangaroo in this picture, have a pouch. The baby is born after a very short time – just five weeks for a kangaroo. The tiny baby climbs into the pouch and attaches itself to the nipple inside, where it feeds on milk and grows.

Baby kangaroos are called Joeys. They stay in the pouch for 235 days.

All marsupials have a very short gestation period.

The baby is completely helpless when it climbs into its mother's pouch.

Answers

The mice and blackbirds are completely helpless. They are kept in a nest and fed by the mother or both parents. The pheasant and antelope can walk soon after they are born or hatched. The parent still looks after them but they do not need a nest to grow up in.

You can toucan

Watch birds building their nests and see if you can estimate how long it takes.

Birds are expert nest-builders. Using the picture above, see if you can build a birds nest from things such as twigs, wool and string. How long did it take you? It is strong enough to hold a couple of chickens eggs? How does it compare with a real birds nest?

The Meerkat

Name:	Grey Meerkat or suricate
Scientific name:	Suricata suricatta
Where it lives:	South Africa, Angola, Namibia, South Botswana
Habitat:	Open country with sandy ground firm enough to dig burrows.
Size:	48cms including tail
Feeding habits:	Omnivore – eats many different foods e.g. insects, mice, snakes, roots and fruit.
Senses:	Very good eyesight. Good hearing and sense of smell.
Breeding:	Female gives birth to 2-5 young in a grass lined chamber.
Social life:	Very social. Different families live together in a colony.
Conservation:	Not in danger. Hunted and killed by humans because is believed to carry the disease rabies.

Grey meerkats are good at digging burrows in the sandy soil where they live. The burrows have tunnels about 10cm in diameter and 150cm long, with living chambers lined with grass.

As many as 30 grey meerkats live together in family groups in the burrows. Each set of groups like this is called a colony. The meerkats often share their burrows with other animals, such as squirrels, spring hares and another kind of meerkat. During the day they look for food in an area of up to 200 metres around their burrow, called the home range.

It only takes a few weeks for meerkats to eat up all the food in their home range. They have to move on to a new area and dig another set of burrows.

Meerkats don't seem to mind sharing their burrows with other animals.

Home sweet home?

To us a home means a place of comfort, safety and somewhere we know well. For meerkats and many other animals this is also true. But not all animals need a home like this or even a comfortable place to live. Many animals are happy in very cold or very hot conditions, for example.

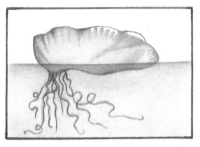

Animals drifting or swimming in the ocean have no need of a home. The Portuguese man-of-war, a kind of jellyfish, drifts for its food.

The arctic fox lives happily in the freezing polar snow. Its fur is so thick that it keeps the fox warm even at -30°C. To rest it digs a shallow pit in the snow.

In the heat of Australia, kangaroos scrape away the top layer of soil and lie in the shallow hollow next to the cooler ground underneath.

Camping out

Some animals just make a very temporary home for hiding and sleeping. Chimpanzees make a new nest up in the trees every night. They bend branches and twigs to form a very loose nest in which they lie down and sleep.

Different kinds of homes serve different purposes. Some animals build homes for their babies. Others build special homes for hunting. The north American beaver builds a very complicated home from logs and branches, called a lodge. It uses its home as a kind of fort to prevent attack by other animals.

Mobile homes

A hermit crab uses an empty snail shell as its home and to protect itself. The crab carries the shell everywhere it goes, but has to find one which fits its body as it grows bigger. When danger is near it hides its legs and claws in the shell.

Ants, bees, wasps and termites are well known for the nests they build. Termite nests can be enormous, with a complicated system of chambers and tunnels. Fresh air circulates around the tunnels – a bit like having an air conditioning system!

Nest builders

The African weaver birds get their name from the way they weave together strands of grass to make complicated nests. Nests like these help protect the eggs and young from attack by predators.

Colonies of weaver birds will build their nests together in one tree.

Burrows

A burrow makes a good home. Staying underground keeps a lemming warm in the wintery arctic, or a desert rat cool in the hot, blazing desert.

Some animals, such as the aardvark, are especially good at making burrows. An aardvark has powerful front legs and claws for digging. They make their burrows on the open savannas of Africa.

Under parts of the American prairies is a vast network of tunnels and chambers.

These underground towns belong to the prairie marmot. Vast colonies of prarie marmots live in these towns.

Trap door

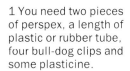

The trap door spider lives in a silk tube during the day. At night, it keeps the trap door slightly open. When an insect comes near, the spider grabs it and drags the victim into its underground tube to eat.

You can toucan

Here is a temporary home for a whole range of animals you might want to look at and keep for a short time, such as worms, insects or pond life.

Make sure you always put the animals back where you found them.

1 You need two pieces of perspex, a length of plastic or rubber tube, four bull-dog clips and some plasticine.

2 Clip the perspex and tube together with the bulldog clips as shown in the picture.

3 Fill the gap between the perspex with water to make a mini aquarium or soil to watch worms make their burrows.

Mix and match

See if you can match these animals with their homes:

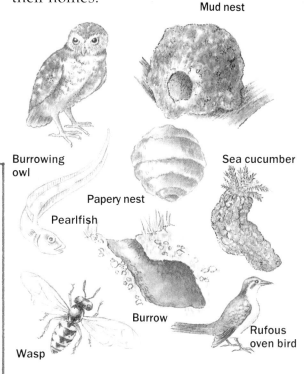

Mud nest

Burrowing owl

Sea cucumber

Papery nest

Pearlfish

Burrow

Rufous oven bird

Wasp

Answers

The rufous oven bird makes a nest from mud. It looks like a clay oven.

Wasps make their nest from plant material. They chew it and make a paper-thin but strong nest of chambers.

The pearlfish lives inside the body of the sea cucumber, which harms the sea cucumber.

The burrowing owl digs a hole in the ground to lay its eggs and rear its young.

Maps

See if you can draw a map of your home range – the area in which you feel safe and happy. This is called your mental map. Ask some friends to do the same thing and see if their maps are similar to yours.

Many animals have a home range area in the same way as the meerkat. The size of the range depends on the animal, but by staying within its boundaries the animal gets to know it very well.

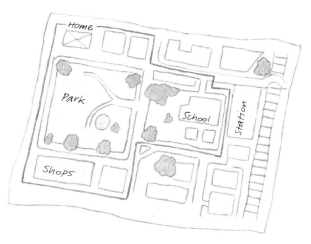

Leafcutter ant

Most ants live together in a large, well organized group, with all the ants depending on each other for survival. There can be as many as two and a half million leafcutter ants living together in a single colony, for example.

Ant society is divided into different classes, called castes. At the head is the queen, followed by the males. The males mate with the queen, who spends all her life laying eggs. Then there are worker ants who look after the colony. There are three kinds of worker leafcutter ants – large, medium and small.

Name:	Leafcutter or parasol ant
Scientific name:	Atta (several species)
Where it lives:	Tropical and sub-tropical areas of south and central America
Habitat:	Forests and areas of vegetation
Size:	Queen – 1.8cm, male – 1.3cm, largest worker – 1.3cm, smallest worker – 2.5mm
Feeding Habits:	Herbivore – eats a special fungus grown on leaves
Senses:	Touch, smell and taste are the ant's best senses
Breeding:	The queen lays eggs all the time. They are looked after and reared by worker ants
Social Life:	Well organized with different classes doing different jobs
Conservation:	Very common. Can be a pest because it will eat plant leaves growing in plantations

Long sharp jaws used to cut leaves into pieces.

The workers

The large workers protect the colony from attackers. Their long sharp jaws make ideal weapons as well as being good for cutting up leaves. The medium workers cut and carry leaves back to the nest. Finally the smallest workers grow and care for a special fungus garden in the nest. This fungus is the food for all the ants. The leaves are chewed and spat out to make a compost on which the fungus grows.

The smallest workers also ride on the leaves as guards. They do this to protect the other workers from attacks by parasitic flies.

A medium worker ant carrying a piece of leaf back to the nest.

A guard ant fighting off a tiny fly trying to lay an egg on a worker's head. The maggot which hatches out of the fly's egg would eat the ant's brain unless it were protected in this way.

Living in a group

Why do animals live together? Some of the reasons are shown below. See if you can think of any others.

Safety in numbers

Animals in a group have a better chance of escape from predators than individuals. There are many more ears, eyes and noses to spot danger.

Comfort and joy

Social animals can rely on each other for comfort and support. Baboons and many other mammals take great delight in grooming and being groomed.

Sharing the work

Groups of animals usually share the workload. One female meerkat, for example, acts as a babysitter while the others go off looking for food. Another may do guard duty and keep a look out for danger while the rest are feeding.

Learning about life

Animals can learn from the actions of others in a group. An intelligent Macaque monkey in Japan worked out how to wash sand off potatoes given to her by some people. All the others learnt this from her. Generations of these monkeys still wash their potatoes in the same way as the original monkey.

Sacrifice

Naked mole rats live in an underground colony with a queen, workers and soldiers, just like ants. They move around in the tunnels in a long line, with the smallest at the end of the line. If an attacker, such as a snake gets into the burrow, the little one squeaks a warning to the others. They block up the burrow to keep the snake out, but the small naked mole rat usually gets caught and eaten. It gives up its life to help the colony.

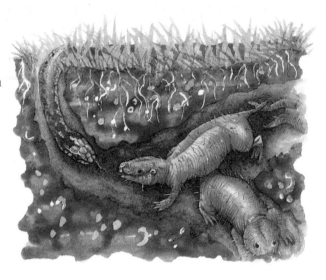

Pecking orders

Many animals in groups have a pecking order, which works like this:

1 At the top there is a powerful animal who is the leader. This animal can peck any of the others.

2 Then there is a weaker animal who can peck anyone but the leader.

3 Next comes another animal who can peck anyone but the animals above it.

4 Right at the end there is a much weaker animal with no power who gets pecked by everyone.

The animal at the bottom of the pecking order never has the best food, loses all the fights and becomes very nervous. Living in a group is good for most individuals, but not all animals in the group do well from it.

Lazy lions?

A male lion seems to have a lazy life. He hardly ever joins in the killing of his prey, but always has first pick of the meal. But even if he is the leader he too has to make some sacrifices. He must fight other males who want to take over his pride. This gets more difficult as he gets older. Eventually he may be chased away or killed by a younger, stronger lion.

Bodyguards

A group of baboons is called a troop. The troop is headed by one male who is the leader. Within the group there are young males and females, mothers with babies and with young animals. The other adult males follow the troop as it wanders around the open plains of Africa and provide protection.

The boss

Like baboons, gorillas have several males, females and young living together. Once again there is one dominant animal in the group. He is always a male and you can recognize him from his silver-coloured back.

Breeding groups

Some groups only come together during the breeding season. When deer want to breed, male deer fight with one another and gather together a group of females. They stay together long enough to mate. After the breeding season, the males go off together in large groups called stag parties. They stay together until the next breeding season.

You can toucan

You are a social animal living in a group called human society. Try making a list of all the people who you rely on to help you every day. Do other people rely on you too?

Perhaps you could think about how you can help others in your society.

Here is a pecking order puzzle to work out.

Dozy can peck Beaky.

Fluff can peck Dozy and Beaky.

Beaky can't peck Feathers and neither can Dozy.

Feathers can peck Fluff. What is the pecking order?

Answer: Feathers, Fluff, Dozy, Beaky

Barn Owl

The barn owl is one of nature's most beautiful hunters – a silent, stealthy killing machine. It is one of the most widespread birds in the world, yet in Great Britain it is a very rare species. The barn owl is rare in Britain for three main reasons: its habitat has changed, it has been hunted and also killed by poisonous chemicals.

Soft, fine feathers which do not make a noise when the owl flies.

Very sensitive hearing.

Large eyes to see in the dark.

A hooked beak for tearing at flesh.

Name:	Barn owl
Scientific name:	Tyto alba
Where it lives:	Europe, America, Africa, India, south east Asia and Australia
Habitat:	Desert to tropical forests
Size:	335 centimetres
Feeding habits:	Carnivore — eats small animals: mice, rats and birds
Senses:	Very good eyesight and hearing
Breeding:	4-7 eggs laid in a hollow tree or an old building
Social life:	Solitary except at breeding time
Conservation:	Common throughout the world but rare in Great Britain

Powerful talons for gripping and crushing its prey.

40

A changing habitat

As the countryside is made tidier, old barns and dead trees are pulled down. This means there are fewer places for the barn owl to nest. One way that people can encourage barn owls is to put up owl nesting boxes.

Barn owls often fly near motorways, hunting for small voles and mice along the verges. They fly very low and are sometimes killed accidently by cars.

Hunting

Some people killed barn owls thinking they attacked game birds. In fact, barn owls hunt pests that eat crops such as mice, rats and birds. Hunting barn owls is now against the law.

Pollution

Chemicals are sprayed on to crops to kill pests. Mice and other small animals eat these crops. In their turn, they are eaten by owls. The chemicals build up in the owl's body, making it sick. Some owls have so many chemicals inside them that they cannot lay proper eggs. This means that they cannot breed to increase their numbers.

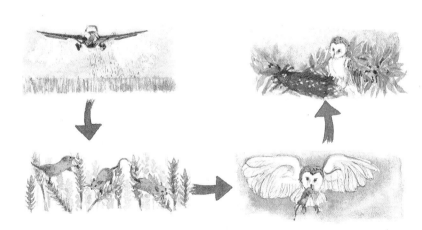

There are also chemicals which poison and kill barn owls directly. Some chemicals are so dangerous that they are banned.

Going

The giant panda feeds on almost nothing else but bamboo, but many of the forests where it lives have been destroyed. Bamboo plants flower about every 100 years, and this happened in the early 1980s. Not enough new bamboo shoots grew, so many pandas starved to death. People from around the world are working very hard to help save the giant panda.

Going

The blue whale has been hunted so much for the oils in its body that nobody is now really sure how many are left alive. In one year alone as many as 29,000 blue whales were killed. They are now no longer hunted, so perhaps their numbers will increase.

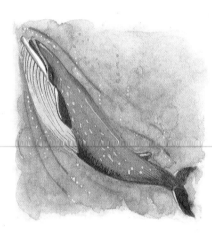

Gone

The dodo, a flightless bird, lived on an island called Mauritius in the Indian Ocean. Vistiting 17th century sailors killed the dodo to eat. Rats escaped from the sailor's boats and probably ate the dodo's eggs and killed its young. The dodo is now extinct. No one will ever see a living dodo again. We only know what they looked like from drawings made in the 1600s.

A second chance

Some animals, such as the Arabian oryx, were hunted to extinction in the wild. A few animals in zoos were left. They were brought together during the 1960s to breed and a small captive herd survived. In the 1980s they were gradually released in to the wild.

The mountain gorilla

Nature reserves or national parks are sometimes created to help conserve wild animals and wild places. In Rwanda, a small African country, tourists visit the famous national park to watch mountain gorillas. A farmer in Rwanda can earn more money from selling things to tourists than he would from farming. So the farmers in the area are helping to save the gorillas by giving some land.

Farming for conservation

One way to conserve wild animals is to farm them. In tropical parts of the world butterflies, crocodiles, iguanas and turtles are all farmed. Selling the animals for their skins or as food helps earn money for the local people and stops the hunting of the animals in the wild.

Think carefully

Wildlife conservation means thinking carefully about our environment before making any changes. Human beings are a part of nature and never separate from it. If we do not find ways of living with wildlife instead of destroying it, we risk destroying ourselves.

Here are four animals that are hunted and used by people in some way. Try to work out what they might be used for just by looking at them. The answers are below:

Many species of wild cats are hunted and killed for their fur for use as coats. If people stopped wearing these coats then there would be no need to kill the cats.

All species of rhinoceros are very rare. Although protected by law some people break these laws and kill the rhinos for their horns. They are ground down to powder and sold as medicine, or carved for dagger handles.

Coral is formed from chalky material made by the tiny coral animals. Explosives are used to blow up the coral reef. The coral is used for building material. Sometimes small pieces are sold to tourists.

It is illegal to catch some kinds of monkeys. But still many are caught and smuggled to be sold as pets, or used for scientific research.

Grouping game

The ten selected animals can be put in to different groups depending on the features they have. To play the grouping game look at the features you can easily see. Match them with a description below. If you are still not sure which animal fits in to which group look at the list of features you can't easily see. You can then check that information with what you can find out about the animal in other parts of the book. If you get really stuck, the answers are below.

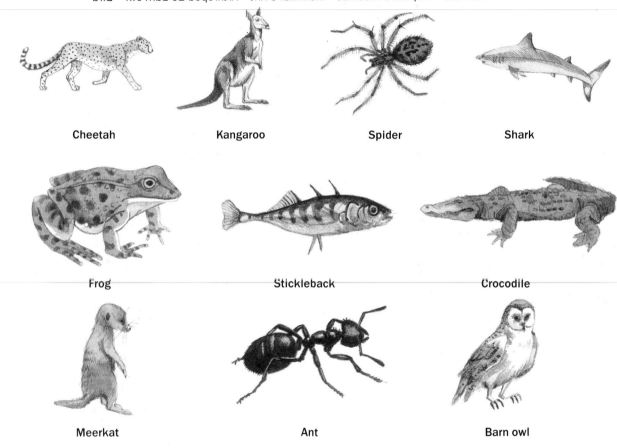

Cheetah   Kangaroo   Spider   Shark

Frog   Stickleback   Crocodile

Meerkat   Ant   Barn owl

Quiz extra

You could try grouping these animals too, but they are more difficult. Look very closely at them. Which group does each of these belong to?

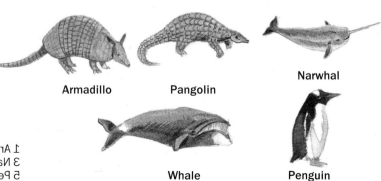

Armadillo   Pangolin   Narwhal

Whale   Penguin

Name of Group	Features you can easily see	Features you can't easily see
Mammal	Fur/hair and most have ear flaps	Has a backbone and is warm blooded. Gives birth to live young and feeds them on milk. Breathes air.
Bird	Has feathers and a beak	Has a backbone and is warm blooded. Lays hard shelled eggs in some kind of nest. Breathes air.
Reptile	Has dry, scaly skin	Has a backbone but is cold blooded. Lays eggs with a softer shell than birds. Breathes air.
Amphibian	Has a smooth, moist, sometimes slimy skin	Has a backbone but is coldblooded. Lays small, soft, eggs in water. Breathes air.
Fish	Has a scaly skin, fins and lives in water	There are two very big groups of fish, the bony and the cartilaginous fish. The bony fish have a gill cover; the cartilaginous fish have gill slits.
	Fish have a tail flattened from side to side which moves sideways	Has a backbone and breathes water through gills. Bony fish have a bony skeleton inside their body. Cartilaginous fish have a skeleton made from a softer kind of bone called cartilage.
Arthropod	Have a hard outside Armour-like and jointed legs There are many different kinds of arthropods. Count the number of legs to find out which kind of arthropod you are looking at. There should be six legs for insects and eight for spiders and scorpions.	They do not have a backbone. The hard outside is called an external skeleton. Some breathe air, others breathe water.

Wildlife map

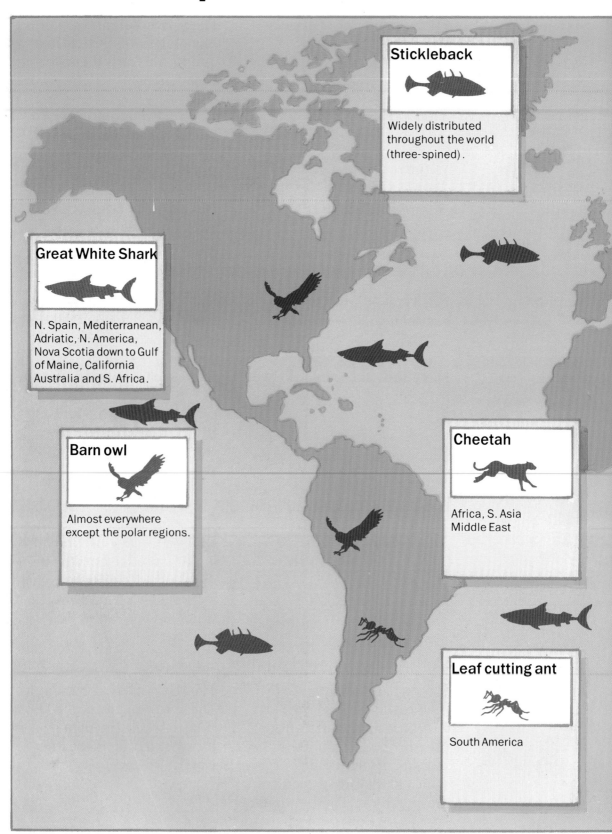

Stickleback

Widely distributed throughout the world (three-spined).

Great White Shark

N. Spain, Mediterranean, Adriatic, N. America, Nova Scotia down to Gulf of Maine, California Australia and S. Africa.

Barn owl

Almost everywhere except the polar regions.

Cheetah

Africa, S. Asia Middle East

Leaf cutting ant

South America

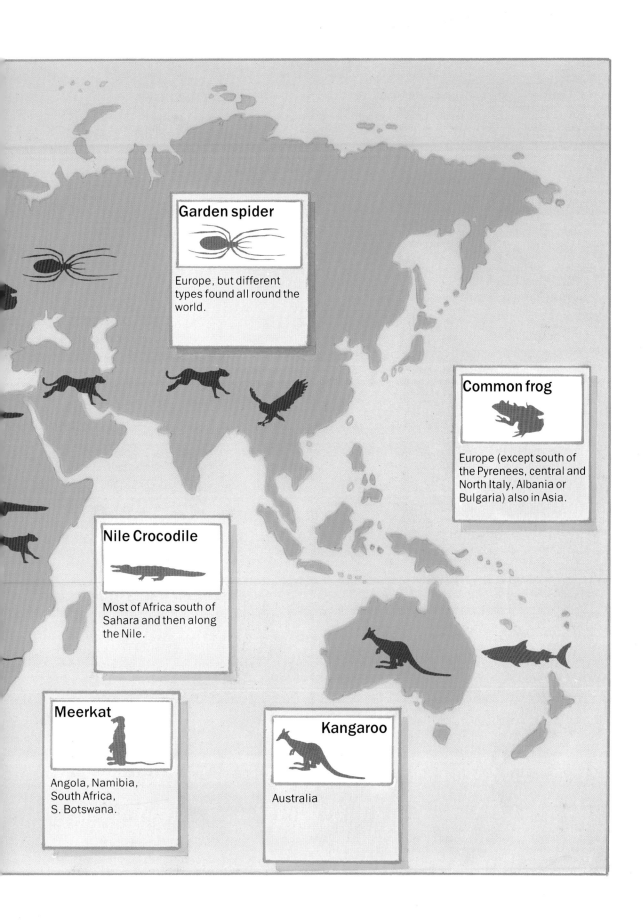

Garden spider

Europe, but different types found all round the world.

Common frog

Europe (except south of the Pyrenees, central and North Italy, Albania or Bulgaria) also in Asia.

Nile Crocodile

Most of Africa south of Sahara and then along the Nile.

Meerkat

Angola, Namibia, South Africa, S. Botswana.

Kangaroo

Australia

Index

Published by BBC Books, a division of BBC Enterprises Limited,
Woodlands, 80 Wood Lane, London W12 0TT

First published 1989, Reprinted 1989

Devised and produced by Tony Potter for BBC Enterprises Limited

Paperback ISBN: 0 563 34162 9
Hardback ISBN: 0 563 34354 0

Picture credits
cover (left) Luke Finn (right) Tony Potter/Ansty Wildlife **p11** (top) Steve
Pollock (bottom) Nature Photographers Ltd **p17** (left) Tony Potter (centre)
Tony Potter (right) S.C. Bisserot/Nature Photographers Ltd **p19** (top left)
Paul Sterry/Nature Photographers Ltd (top right) Steve Pollock (bottom
left) Steve Pollock (bottom right) Tony Potter/Ansty Wildlife **p20** (top) Paul
Sterry/Nature Photographers Ltd (bottom) Colin Carver/Nature
Photographers Ltd **p25** (left) Steve Pollock (right) Tony Potter **p37** L.H.
Brown/Nature Photographers Ltd **p43** Steve Pollock

Typeset by TDR, Dartford, England
Origination by Dot Gradations, England

Printed in Great Britain by BPCC Paulton Books Limited